1001
Things to Spot
in the Sea

Katie Daynes and Susanna Davidson

Illustrated by Teri Gower

Designed by Natacha Goransky and Anna Gould

Natural history consultants: Dr. Margaret Rostron
and Dr. John Rostron

Usborne Quicklinks

For links to websites with video clips, activities and amazing facts about life in the seas and oceans, go to the Usborne Quicklinks website at www.usborne.com/quicklinks and enter the keywords '1001 sea'. Please follow the internet safety guidelines at the Usborne Quicklinks website. We recommend that children are supervised while on the internet.

Contents

How to use this book

The scenes in this book show seas and oceans from around the world. In each scene there are lots of things for you to find and count. There is also a puzzle on pages 34 to 35 with even more things to spot in the sea. There are 1001 things to spot in this book altogether.

The number shows you how many
of that thing you need to find.

Icy north

The Arctic Ocean is the coldest in the world and is frozen for most of the year. In winter it is dark all the time, while in summer the sun never sets. Few animals can survive here all year round, but in summer its waters teem with life.

10 capelin   4 Arctic terns   8 ringed seals   10 harp seals   8 harp seal pups

4 polar bears   9 Arctic cod   5 white parkas   3 killer whales   9 Arctic char

The icons show
you what to look
for in each scene.

Look at the
world map
to see where
each scene
takes place.

This is Billy. He has explored seas and oceans all over the world, and always takes his underwater camera with him. Can you spot his camera in every scene?

5

Map of the oceans

More than two-thirds of the world is covered by seas and oceans. This map shows the five different oceans around the world.

By the seashore,
pages 16-17

Water sports,
pages 10-11

ATLANTIC OCEAN

Underwater
forest,
pages 18-19

Grassy seabed,
pages 30-31

On a cruise,
pages 20-21

Open ocean,
pages 8-9

Deep down,
pages 22-23

PACIFIC OCEAN

SOUTHERN OCEAN

ARCTIC OCEAN

Icy north,
pages 12-13

PACIFIC OCEAN

Lost city,
pages 26-27

Shipwreck,
pages 32-33

Sea village,
pages 24-25

INDIAN OCEAN

Coral reef,
pages 14-15

Chilly south,
pages 28-29

Open ocean

Far out, beyond the shore, lies the open ocean. Schools of fish gather near the sunlit surface and sharks come to feed on them. Birds divebomb from above, while turtles chase jellyfish through the rolling waves.

8

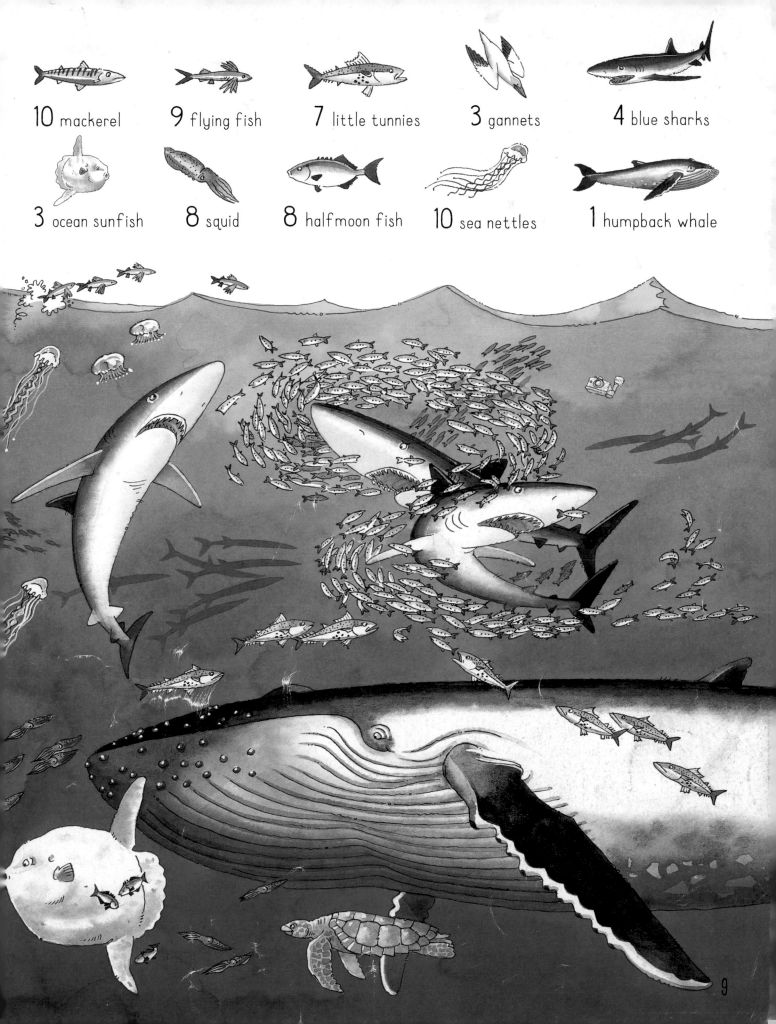

10 mackerel

9 flying fish

7 little tunnies

3 gannets

4 blue sharks

3 ocean sunfish

8 squid

8 halfmoon fish

10 sea nettles

1 humpback whale

9

Water sports

As the wind blows across the water, ripples turn into waves. Children ride boogie boards into shore while, further out, windsurfers catch the breeze in their sails and skim across the surface of the sea.

9 red buoys

6 striped sails

10 herring gulls

5 windsurfers

7 boogie boards

4 speedboats

10 flippers

5 jet skis

9 yellow life jackets

3 rubber rings

Icy north

The Arctic Ocean is the coldest in the world and is frozen for most of the year. In winter it is dark all the time, while in summer the sun never sets. Few animals can survive here all year round, but in summer its waters teem with life.

10 capelin

4 Arctic terns

8 ringed seals

10 harp seals

8 harp seal pups

4 polar bears

9 Arctic cod

5 white parkas

3 killer whales

9 Arctic char

Coral reef

Scattered through Earth's shallow, sunlit waters, coral reefs are home to thousands of different plants and animals. But watch out! The creatures here are beautiful, but often deadly.

10 clown fish

7 feather stars

4 brain corals

5 groupers

6 porcupine fish

9 dart fish

8 sea slugs

10 angel fish

5 giant clams

9 trigger fish

By the seashore

When the tide goes out, there are lots of things to spot on the seashore. People come for picnics and to look for creatures in the pools of water trapped among the rocks. Shorebirds flock to the beach, too, looking for tasty snacks to eat.

8 oystercatchers 4 sandwiches 5 fishing nets 7 hermit crabs 9 groups of mussels

3 blue sunhats 10 gobies 8 shore crabs 6 black-headed gulls 8 red buckets

Underwater forest

Along the coast, forests of kelp provide a home for many different animals. Some use the forests as a nursery for their young or for shelter. For others it makes the perfect hunting ground.

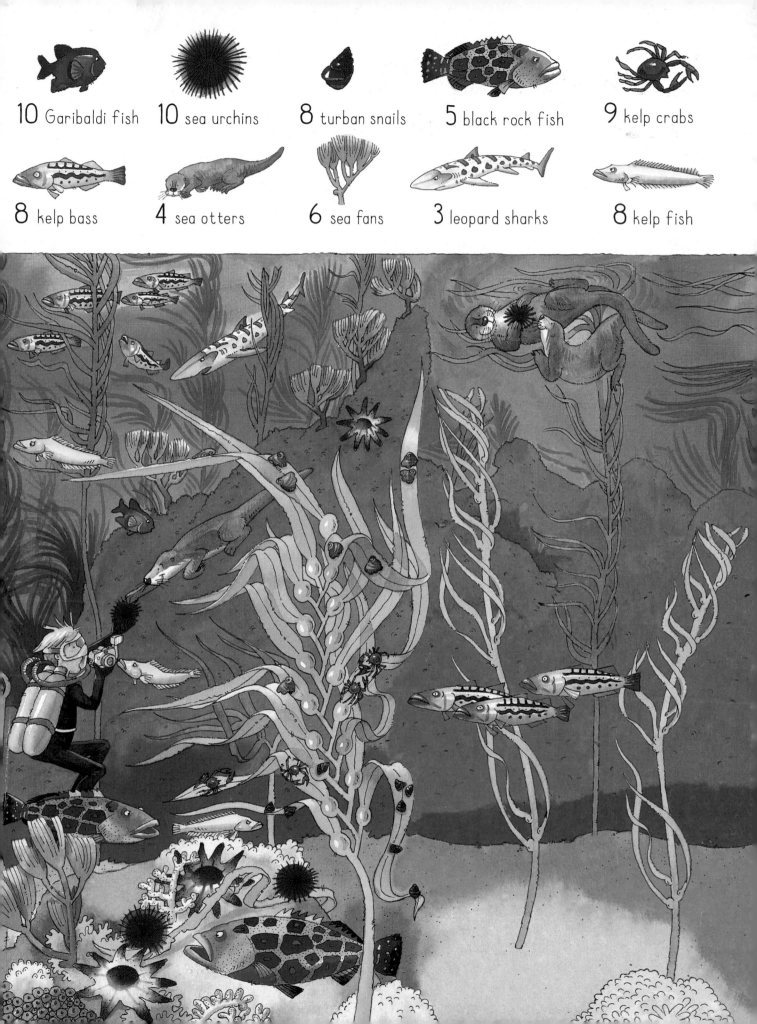

10 Garibaldi fish **10** sea urchins **8** turban snails **5** black rock fish **9** kelp crabs

8 kelp bass **4** sea otters **6** sea fans **3** leopard sharks **8** kelp fish

On a cruise

Huge ships sail the oceans, carrying people and goods around the world. Cruise ships are among the biggest. They are like floating hotels, with bedrooms, restaurants and swimming pools. Dolphins like to ride the waves along the bow.

3 lifeboats

7 life rings

8 deck lights

5 tables

6 yellow loungers

4 yachts

10 palm trees

8 striped loungers

9 ship's officers

4 pairs of binoculars

21

Deep down

The deeper you go, the darker it gets. Strange creatures lurk on the ocean floor – fanged fish that make their own light, eels with enormous mouths and octopuses with fins on the tops of their heads that look like flappy ears.

10 lantern fish

9 vent shrimp

10 vent crabs

5 dumbo octopuses

1 submersible

7 black smokers

5 gulper eels

6 angler fish

9 deep-sea jellyfish

8 spook fish

Sea village

Sea gypsies live in bamboo houses on stilts off the west coast of Thailand, in the Andaman Sea. Many make their living by fishing or diving for pearls, in hand-built wooden boats called kabang.

24

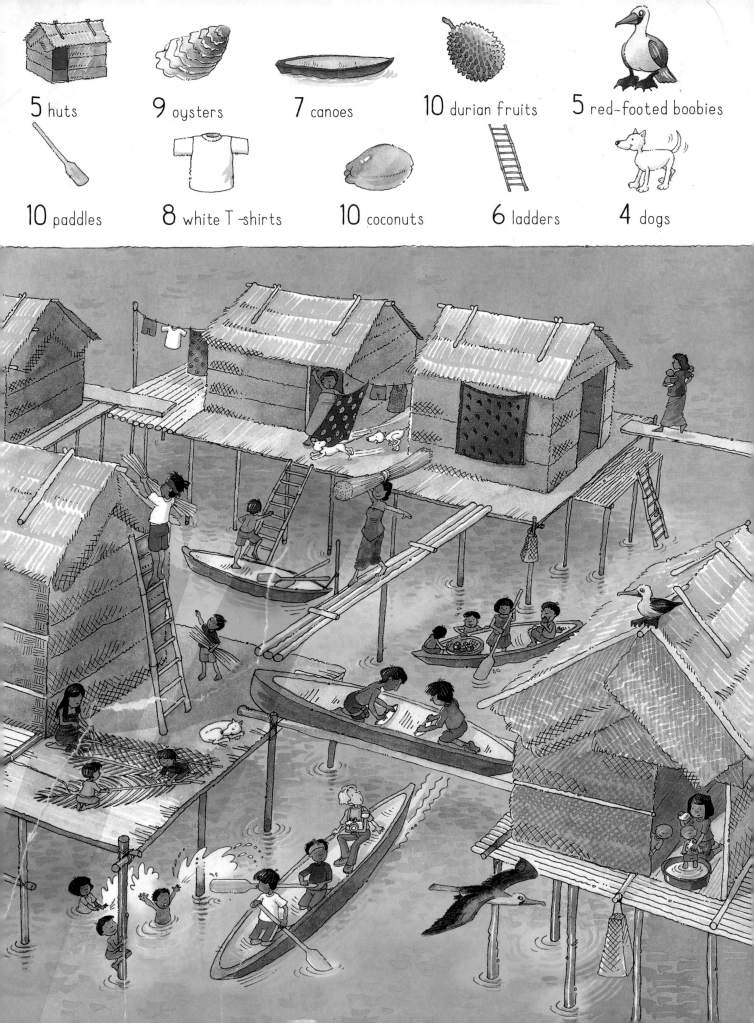

5 huts

9 oysters

7 canoes

10 durian fruits

5 red-footed boobies

10 paddles

8 white T-shirts

10 coconuts

6 ladders

4 dogs

Lost city

Beneath the waves of the Mediterranean Sea lies the lost city of Heracleion, which once served as a port of entry to Egypt. Now divers search for gold coins, statues and buried ships. Many sea creatures have made this sunken city their home.

9 greeneye fish

6 jars

7 seabream

7 gold coins

7 divers

10 cardinal fish

6 octopuses

9 whelk shells

10 bullet tuna

1 white stone head

27

Chilly south

The Southern Ocean surrounds Antarctica. Every spring, penguins make their nests along its rocky shores, while seals come ashore to breed. Whales swim through its cold waters, feasting on plankton and fish.

1 whale-watchers' tour 6 backpacks 5 elephant seals 9 chinstrap penguins 8 albatrosses

3 whale tails 10 king penguins 10 penguin chicks 9 brown skuas 4 hourglass dolphins

Grassy seabed

Mangrove trees have their roots in salty water, providing a sheltered home for fish and crabs, and a perfect feeding ground for water birds. Sea grasses grow along the muddy floor, browsed on by manatees.

10 mullet

8 yellow winkles

8 catfish

3 manatees

10 butterfly fish

7 seeds

6 roseate spoonbills

9 snappers

8 blue crabs

7 terrapins

Shipwreck

Far beneath the waves are sunken ships, some hundreds of years old, waiting to be discovered. Divers come with breathing tanks and waterproof paper, to draw what they have seen.

9 barracudas

5 carnation corals

9 squirrel fish

1 anchor

10 surgeon fish

9 sweetlips

2 writing slates

9 banner fish

4 moray eels

7 cow fish

More things to spot

Billy has photographed sea creatures from every scene in this book. Look back through the pages and see if you can find and count all these animals.

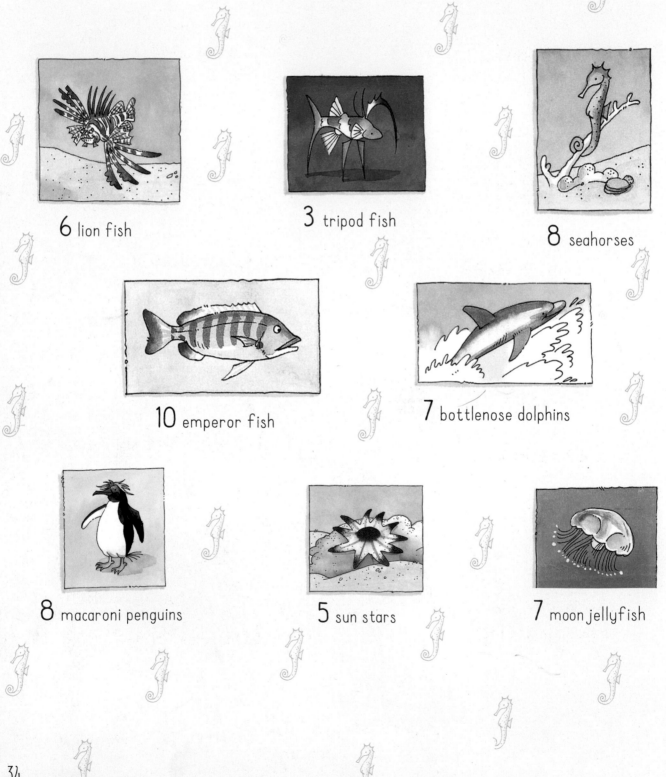

6 lion fish

3 tripod fish

8 seahorses

10 emperor fish

7 bottlenose dolphins

8 macaroni penguins

5 sun stars

7 moon jellyfish

6 spiny lobsters

10 walruses

7 butterfly blennies

10 red sea anemones

2 Napoleon wrasses

9 Picasso trigger fish

1 blue-spotted ray

3 loggerhead turtles

Habitats

The seas and oceans are made up of lots of different kinds of habitats, from rock pools to tropical reefs. Each animal is perfectly suited to its habitat. Here are some examples:

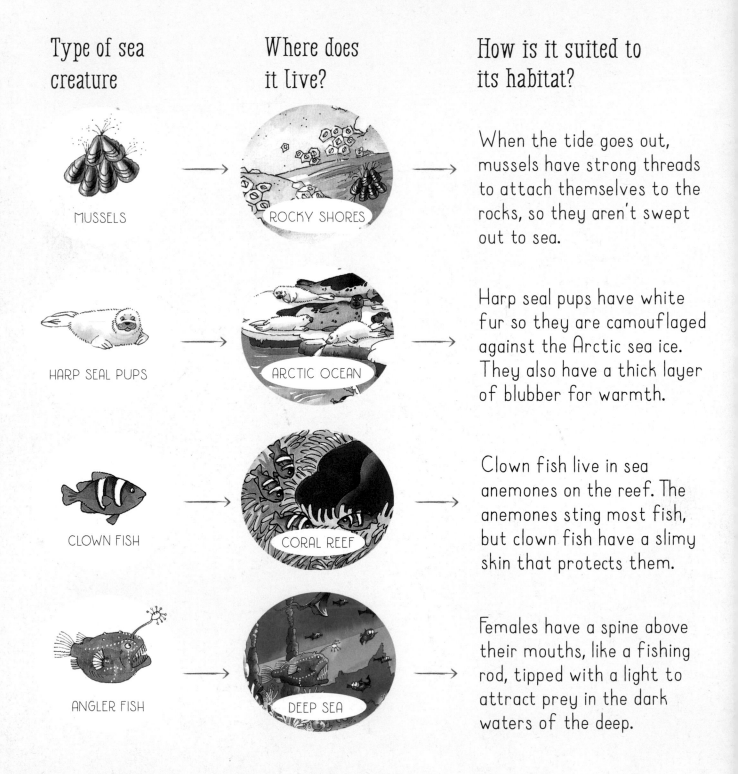

Type of sea creature	Where does it live?	How is it suited to its habitat?
MUSSELS	ROCKY SHORES	When the tide goes out, mussels have strong threads to attach themselves to the rocks, so they aren't swept out to sea.
HARP SEAL PUPS	ARCTIC OCEAN	Harp seal pups have white fur so they are camouflaged against the Arctic sea ice. They also have a thick layer of blubber for warmth.
CLOWN FISH	CORAL REEF	Clown fish live in sea anemones on the reef. The anemones sting most fish, but clown fish have a slimy skin that protects them.
ANGLER FISH	DEEP SEA	Females have a spine above their mouths, like a fishing rod, tipped with a light to attract prey in the dark waters of the deep.

Web of life

The animals in the oceans depend on each other to survive. Some animals eat plants, while others hunt and eat other animals. Food webs, like this one, show how animals are linked together by what they eat. The arrows point from the prey to the predators.

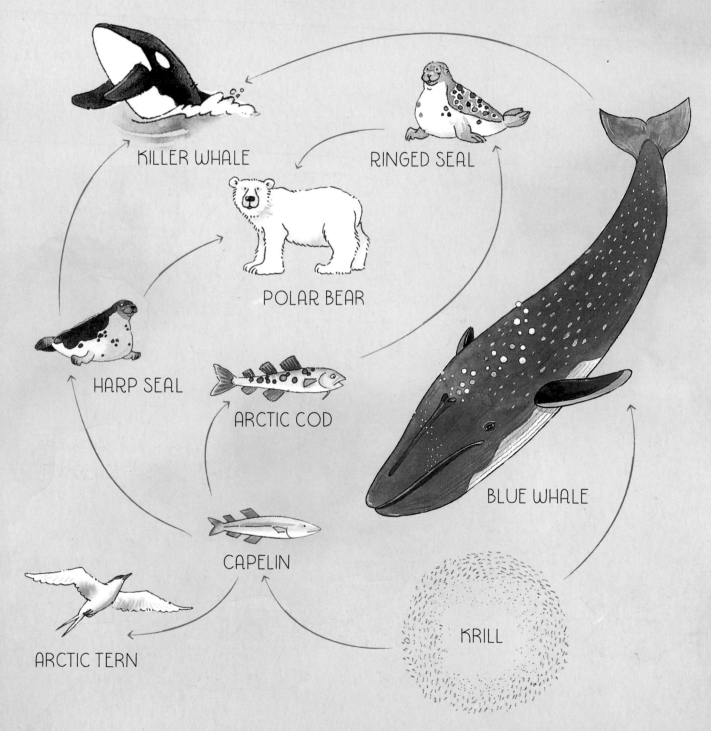

KILLER WHALE

RINGED SEAL

POLAR BEAR

HARP SEAL

ARCTIC COD

BLUE WHALE

CAPELIN

KRILL

ARCTIC TERN

Did you know...?

Here are amazing facts about some of the things to spot in this book.

 ARCTIC TERNS make the longest journey of any animal, from the Arctic to the Antarctic and back again each year – a round trip of around 90,000 km (55,923 miles).

 POLAR BEARS are the largest living land carnivores on Earth. Adults can measure over 2.5 m (8 ft) long and weigh around 680 kg (1,499 lbs).

 GULPER EELS have mouths bigger than their bodies and can swallow animals much larger than themselves.

 GIANT CLAMS fasten themselves to a spot on the reef and stay there for life. They can live for one hundred years or more.

 HERMIT CRABS use abandoned snail shells as homes for their soft bodies. As they outgrow their shells, they leave them and move into bigger ones.

 SEA OTTERS have denser fur than any other animal on Earth – an estimated 1 million hairs per square inch.

DURIAN FRUIT smell so bad they are banned from Singapore's railways.

OCTOPUSES are the most intelligent invertebrates on Earth. They have been known to use tools, can open childproof pill bottles and can camouflage themselves in just three-tenths of a second.

MALE ELEPHANT SEALS can inflate their bulbous noses, to make their snorts and grunts much louder, in order to show off in front of females.

Answers

Did you find all the photographed sea creatures in the book?
Here's where they are:

7 moon jellyfish: Open ocean (pages 8-9)

10 emperor fish: Sea village (pages 24-25)

8 seahorses: Grassy seabed (pages 30-31)

7 bottlenose dolphins: On a cruise (pages 20-21)

9 Picasso fish: Coral reef (pages 14-15)

6 spiny lobsters: Grassy seabed (pages 30-31)

10 walruses: Icy north (pages 12-13)

8 macaroni penguins: Chilly south (pages 28-29)

10 red sea anemones: By the seashore (pages 16-17)

2 Napoleon wrasses: Shipwreck (pages 32-33)

7 butterfly blennies: Lost city (pages 26-27)

5 sun stars: Underwater forest (pages 18-19)

1 blue-spotted ray: Shipwreck (pages 32-33)

3 loggerhead turtles: Open ocean (pages 8-9)

Index

Digital artworking and retouching by Mike Olley and John Russell

Edited by Anna Milbourne and Jane Chisholm
The publishers would like to thank the following people for their advice: Emad Khalil, underwater archaeologist at
Southampton University; Jonathan Mendez, chief powerboat instructor for the Royal Yachting Association;
Rachael Saul from Hebridean Cruises Ltd.; Matt Slater, marine biologist at Blue Reef Aquarium, Newquay;
Sally Thomas at the Royal Institute of Naval Architects